14.95

DATE DUE

DEMCO, INC. 38-2931

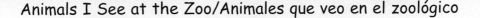

Animals I See at the Zoo/Animales que veo en el zoológico

PEACOCKS/ PAVOS REALES

by/por Kathleen Pohl

Reading consultant: Susan Nations, M.Ed., author/literacy coach/consultant in literacy development

Consultora de lectura: Susan Nations, M.Ed., autora/tutora de alfabetización/ consultora de desarrollo de la lectura

WEEKLY READER®
PUBLISHING

Please visit our web site at: www.garethstevens.com
For a free color catalog describing our list of high-quality
books, call 1-800-542-2595 (USA) or 1-800-387-3178 (Canada).

Library of Congress Cataloging-in-Publication Data

Pohl, Kathleen.
   [Peacocks. Spanish & English]
   Peacocks/Pavos reales / Kathleen Pohl.
      p. cm. — (Animals I see at the zoo/Animales que veo en el zoologico)
   ISBN-10: 0-8368-8235-0 (lib. bdg.)
   ISBN-13: 978-0-8368-8235-3 (lib. bdg.)
   ISBN-10: 0-8368-8242-3 (softcover)
   ISBN-13: 978-0-8368-8242-1 (softcover)
    1. Peafowl—Juvenile literature. I. Title. II. Title: Pavos reales.
   QL696.G27P6518   2007
   598.6'258—dc22
                                2007021296

This edition first published in 2008 by
Weekly Reader® Books
An imprint of Gareth Stevens Publishing
1 Reader's Digest Road
Pleasantville, NY 10570-7000 USA

Copyright © 2008 by Gareth Stevens, Inc.

Editor: Dorothy L. Gibbs
Art direction: Tammy West
Graphic designer: Charlie Dahl
Photo research: Diane Laska-Swanke
Spanish translation: Tatiana Acosta and Guillermo Gutiérrez

Photo credits: Cover, p. 5 © James P. Rowan; title, p. 9 © Photos.com; p. 7 © Michael
Melford/National Geographic Image Collection; p. 11 © Adam Jones/Visuals Unlimited;
p. 13 © Larry Michael/naturepl.com; p. 15 © Glenn Oliver/Visuals Unlimited; p. 17 © Renee
Purse/Photo Researchers, Inc.; p. 19 © Art Wolfe/Photo Researchers, Inc.; p. 21 © William
Weber/Visuals Unlimited

Printed in the United States of America

1 2 3 4 5 6 7 8 9 11 10 09 08 07

Note to Educators and Parents

Reading is such an exciting adventure for young children! They are beginning to integrate their oral language skills with written language. To encourage children along the path to early literacy, books must be colorful, engaging, and interesting; they should invite the young reader to explore both the print and the pictures.

The *Animals I See at the Zoo* series is designed to help children read about the fascinating animals they might see at a zoo. In each book, young readers will learn interesting facts about the featured animal.

Each book is specially designed to support the young reader in the reading process. The familiar topics are appealing to young children and invite them to read — and re-read — again and again. The full-color photographs and enhanced text further support the student during the reading process.

In addition to serving as wonderful picture books in schools, libraries, homes, and other places where children learn to love reading, these books are specifically intended to be read within an instructional guided reading group. This small group setting allows beginning readers to work with a fluent adult model as they make meaning from the text. After children develop fluency with the text and content, the books can be read independently. Children and adults alike will find these books supportive, engaging, and fun!

— Susan Nations, M.Ed., author, literacy coach,
and consultant in literacy development

Nota para los maestros y los padres

¡Leer es una aventura tan emocionante para los niños pequeños! A esta edad están comenzando a integrar su manejo del lenguaje oral con el lenguaje escrito. Para animar a los niños en el camino de la lectura incipiente, los libros deben ser coloridos, estimulantes e interesantes; deben invitar a los jóvenes lectores a explorar la letra impresa y las ilustraciones.

Animales que veo en el zoológico es una colección diseñada para ayudar a los jóvenes lectores a conocer a los fascinantes animales que pueden ver en un zoológico. En cada libro, los niños leerán interesantes datos sobre un animal.

Cada libro está especialmente diseñado para ayudar a los jóvenes lectores en el proceso de lectura. Los temas familiares llaman la atención de los niños y los invitan a leer una y otra vez. Las fotografías a todo color y el tamaño de la letra ayudan aún más al estudiante en el proceso de lectura.

Además de servir como maravillosos libros ilustrados en escuelas, bibliotecas, hogares y otros lugares donde los niños aprenden a amar la lectura, estos libros han sido especialmente concebidos para ser leídos en un grupo de lectura guiada. Este contexto permite que los lectores incipientes trabajen con un adulto que domina la lectura mientras van determinando el significado del texto. Una vez que los niños dominan el texto y el contenido, el libro puede ser leído de manera independiente. ¡Estos libros les resultarán útiles, estimulantes y divertidos a niños y a adultos por igual!

— Susan Nations, M.Ed., autora/tutora de alfabetización/
consultora de desarrollo de la lectura

I like to go to the zoo.
I see **peacocks** at the zoo.

- - - - - - - - - - - - - -

Me gusta ir al zoológico.
En el zoológico veo
pavos reales.

Peacocks are big birds
with pretty tail feathers.

‐ ‐ ‐ ‐ ‐ ‐ ‐ ‐ ‐ ‐ ‐ ‐ ‐ ‐ ‐

Los pavos reales son unas
aves grandes con bellas
plumas en la cola.

tail feathers/
plumas de
la cola

They spread out their tail
feathers like **fancy** fans.

-- -- -- -- -- -- -- -- -- -- --

Los pavos reales
despliegan las plumas
de la cola como si fuera
un **vistoso** abanico.

Do you see lots of eyes?
A peacock's tail feathers
have large spots on them.
The spots look like eyes!

--- --- --- --- --- --- --- --- --- --- ---

¿Ves muchos ojos? Las
plumas de la cola de un
pavo real tienen grandes
manchas. ¡Las manchas
parecen ojos!

eyespots/
manchas con
forma de ojo

11

Look at all the bright colors — blue and green and gold! They **sparkle** in the sunlight.

¡Mira todos esos brillantes colores: azul, verde, dorado! Mira cómo **centellean** al sol.

When a peacock closes
its fan, the long feathers
drag on the ground!

Cuando un pavo real
pliega la cola, ¡arrastra
sus largas plumas por
el suelo!

Peacocks spend most of the day on the ground. They eat grain, bugs, and berries.

- - - - - - - - - - - - - - -

Los pavos reales pasan la mayor parte del día en el suelo. Comen granos, insectos y bayas.

At night, they fly into trees to sleep.

Por la noche, vuelan a los árboles para dormir.

I like to see peacocks
at the zoo. Do you?

- - - - - - - - - - - - - -

Me gusta ver pavos
reales en el zoológico.
¿Y a ti?

Glossary

drag — to trail, or follow, behind

fancy — colorful and decorative

grain — the small seeds of cereal plants such as corn or wheat

peacocks — big birds that are known for their long, colorful tail feathers

sparkle — to shine with sparks of light, like glitter

Glosario

arrastrar — tirar de algo por el suelo

centellear — brillar algo como si emitiera luz

granos — pequeñas semillas de plantas de cereales como el maíz o el trigo

pavos reales — aves grandes conocidas por sus largas y coloridas plumas de la cola

vistoso — colorido y atractivo

For More Information/
Más información

Books/Libros

Berman, Ruth. *Peacocks*. Minneapolis: Lerner, 1996.

Parramon, J. M. and Sales, G. *Mi primera vista al aviario*. Hauppauge, New York: Barron's Juveniles, 1990.

Scheunemann, Pam. *Peacock Fan*. Edina, Minnesota: ABDO, SandCastle, 2006.

Underwood, Deborah. *Colorful Peacocks*. Minneapolis: Lerner, 2006.

Index/Índice

About the Author/Información sobre la autora

Kathleen Pohl has written and edited many children's books, including animal tales, rhyming books, retold classics, and the forty-book series *Nature Close-Ups*. Most recently, she authored the Weekly Reader® leveled reader series *Let's Read About Animals* and *Where People Work*. She also served for many years as top editor of *Taste of Home* and *Country Woman* magazines. She and her husband, Bruce, share their home in the beautiful Wisconsin woods with six goats, a llama, and all kinds of wonderful woodland creatures.

Kathleen Pohl ha escrito y corregido muchos libros infantiles. Entre ellos hay cuentos de animales, libros de rimas, versiones nuevas de cuentos clásicos y la serie de cuarenta libros *Nature Close-Ups*. Más recientemente, Kathleen ha escrito los libros de las colecciones *Conozcamos a los animales* y *¿Dónde trabaja la gente?* de *Weekly Reader*. Además, trabajó durante muchos años como directora de las revistas *Taste of Home* and *Country Woman*. Kathleen vive con su marido, Bruce, en medio de los bellos bosques de Wisconsin. Ambos comparten su hogar con seis cabras, una llama y todo tipo de maravillosos animales del bosque.